flood
THE WORLD REACTS

Paul Bennett

Smart Apple Media

FOREWORD

Disasters affect all of us. At some point in life, everyone has a good chance of either being caught in one or knowing someone who is.

For most people, the disaster may be a car crash or a house fire, and the police, firefighters, or ambulance service will be on hand to help. But for millions of people around the world, disasters happen far more often and are more catastrophic.

Some countries suffer frequent natural disasters such as floods, earthquakes, and droughts. They do not always have the resources to deal with the crisis, and it is usually the poorest people who are the most affected and least able to recover.

War is a man-made disaster that ruins people's lives. The effects of droughts and floods are made worse when there is war.

When people are unable to cope with a disaster, they need the help of relief agencies such as the Red Cross. Relief agencies react quickly to emergencies, bringing help to those in need. Many times, people are not even aware of disasters in other countries until international aid is discussed on the news.

The World Reacts series ties in closely with the work of the International Federation of Red Cross and Red Crescent Societies. The Federation coordinates international disaster relief and promotes development around the world to prevent and alleviate human suffering. There is a Red Cross or Red Crescent society in almost every country of the world. In 1997, we helped 22 million people affected by disasters.

This series will help readers understand the problems faced by people threatened by disaster. It will also explain what can be done to help.

George Weber
Secretary General, International Federation of Red Cross and Red Crescent Societies

◄ *The Red Cross symbol (left) was first created to protect the wounded in war and those who cared for them. The Red Crescent symbol (right) is used by Muslim countries around the world. Both symbols have equal status.*

CONTENTS

Words in **bold** appear in
the glossary on page 31.

WHAT ARE FLOODS?

A flood happens when water from rivers or seas spills onto dry land. A serious flood can put people's lives and property in danger.

Wet weather

The main cause of flooding is extreme weather conditions. Heavy rain swells rivers and makes them overflow their banks. In mountainous areas, snow melts in the spring, filling rivers and streams with water. Floods in coastal areas are mainly caused by tropical storms that create huge waves that flood low-lying areas.

Natural disasters

Floods also happen as a result of natural disasters, such as tsunamis and **landslides**. Earthquakes on the sea floor create huge waves, called tsunamis, that travel across the sea at great speeds and pound shore-lines hundreds of miles away. Landslides carry everything in their path down hill-sides. The **debris** from the slide may block a river, causing it to overflow its banks.

▼ *People wade through a flooded street in Wuxi City in China after torrential rain.*

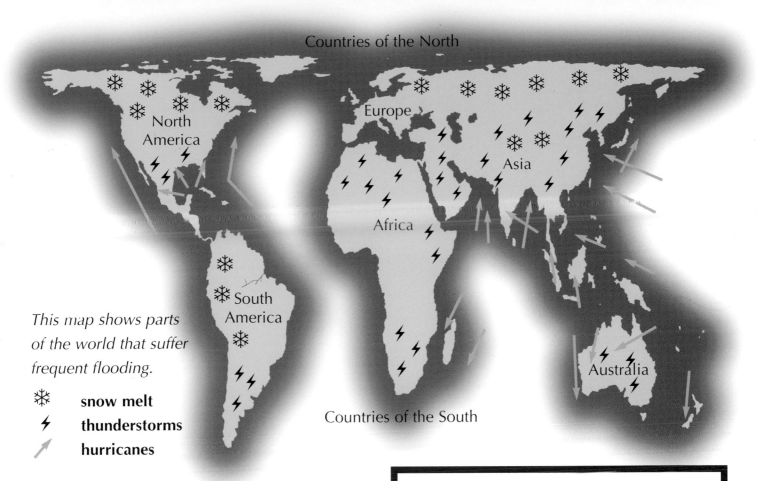

Europe

North America

Asia

Africa

South America

Australia

Countries of the South

This map shows parts of the world that suffer frequent flooding.

❄ **snow melt**

⚡ **thunderstorms**

↗ **hurricanes**

Frequent floods

In some parts of the world, floods are helpful, because they make the soil fertile for farming. For example, Egyptian farmers have relied on the flooding of the Nile River to grow their crops for thousands of years.

In other parts of the world, floods are a constant threat that cause heavy damage and endanger people's lives.

The risk of flooding can be reduced by raising river banks or building barriers. But it is expensive to build flood defenses, and many of the countries most at risk from flooding do not have the money to do it. Some of the worst flood disasters have happened in the world's poorest countries.

The world maps used in this book are called Peters' projection maps. These maps—named after Arno Peters, who designed them—are an accurate way of seeing the world, because they show the actual relative size of continents.

Aid in action

Flood: The World Reacts looks at the disastrous effects a flood can have on towns and cities. It describes recent floods from around the world and examines the help given by governments and **relief agencies**.

This book will help readers understand the problems people face in the days, weeks, and months after a flood. It will also show how the world helps flood victims and suggest how everyone can help.

RIVERS IN FLOOD

People who live near rivers are familiar with the threat of floods caused by heavy rains. From time to time, this flooding causes widespread damage.

Heavy rains

When rain falls to the ground, some of the water soaks into the soil, and some of it runs off the surface into rivers.

When rain is heavy and continues over a long period of time, rivers may not be wide enough or deep enough to hold all of the water. The water rises, flows over the rivers' banks, and floods the land.

In mountainous areas, snow falls in the winter and melts in the spring, filling streams and rivers with water. When heavy rain and a sudden thaw happen at the same time, the water level rises quickly, creating rushing **torrents** of water. When this happens, people are often unaware of the approaching flood until it is too late.

▲ *Water rushes through the village of Vaison-la-Romaine in France in 1992. More than 23 people died in the flood, and the village was completely devastated.*

Wet season

In some parts of the world, the year is divided into wet and dry seasons. During the wet season, rain falls for months at a time, causing rivers to flood. In Asia, this period is called monsoon season. The Ganges River, which flows through India and Bangladesh, regularly floods during this time. People who live near it build their homes on stilts out of the reach of flood waters (left), and farmers plant crops that can withstand flooding.

China 1996

High waters

Large areas of China were hit by severe rainstorms throughout July 1996. Many parts of the country received more than eight inches (20 cm) of rain every day, leading to serious flooding. The Yellow River had its highest water level ever recorded. Powerful storms called typhoons brought more floods, adding to the destruction.

By August 8, nearly 200 million people were affected by the floods. More than 8 million people left their homes, 2,775 were killed, and 234,000 people were sick or injured.

The floods also destroyed the summer rice and grain harvest. With large areas of land flooded, farmers were unable to plant new crops, and food shortages were expected.

▲ *Towns across a large area of China were completely devastated by torrential rain.*

▼ *Hebei Province was one of the most affected areas. Boats were used to rescue trapped people.*

The Chinese government sent in millions of soldiers, policemen, and **volunteers**. They **evacuated** people from their homes, shipped in relief supplies, worked to restore gas and electricity, and tried to control the effects of further flooding.

When the rising waters of the Haihe River threatened the northern city of Tianjin and its population of nine million, the authorities decided to blow up **dikes** to divert the rising river away from the city.

COASTAL FLOODS

Storms and high tides can lead to coastal flooding. Tsunamis caused by earthquakes on the ocean floor may also bring floods.

Storm and tide

The daily rise and fall of the sea are called tides. This difference in sea levels is caused by the pull of the moon and sun. At certain times of the year, when the moon and sun pull together, tides are very high; these are called spring tides.

When there is a high tide and a storm at the same time, the sea level rises. Along low-lying coastlines, the sea floods the land, destroying homes and crops.

When an earthquake happens at sea, the water bulges up into huge waves called tsunamis. In deep water, the waves move across the ocean unseen. But as they reach shallow coastal waters, they rise up as high as 195 feet (60 m) and crash ashore, flooding large areas.

▼ *The awesome power of the sea can be seen as storm waves crash ashore.*

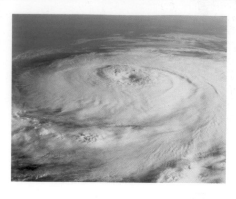

Storm warnings

Storms, such as cyclones, hurricanes, and typhoons, whip up powerful winds and create huge waves. These waves crash ashore and flood low-lying areas. Lives and property can be saved if people are warned of the storm's approach. Weather satellites **orbit** the earth, taking pictures of storms as they develop (above). These satellites also have sensors that detect rain, wind strength, and air temperature. From this information, weather experts can predict the direction of a storm and the areas most at risk from flooding. They can then give warnings to prepare people for the approaching storm.

Vietnam 1997

Typhoon Linda

A delta is an area of land crossed by river channels. They form where the river meets the sea. Many people make their homes near river deltas because the fishing is good and the land is fertile. The Mekong River Delta in Vietnam is a good example, but it, like other deltas, is at risk from flooding from the sea.

▲ *A woman sorts through what is left of her home after Typhoon Linda swept through her village.*

On the night of November 2, 1997, Typhoon Linda tore through the Mekong River Delta, sweeping away more than 80,000 homes, killing 435 people, injuring 833, and leaving more than 3,000 people missing. The typhoon was the worst to strike the area in almost 100 years. In addition to damage to homes, roads, and hospitals, rice fields were flooded, fishing boats were sunk, and shrimp farms were destroyed.

▼ *Rebuilding a dike after it was damaged in the storm.*

Relief supplies, including corrugated iron sheets and wooden poles for making shelters, rice, mosquito nets, and blankets, were taken from the port of Ho Chi Minh to the delta. The supplies were then taken by boat to the communities living along the waterways of the delta. Relief agencies also helped to rebuild or strengthen 500 miles (800 km) of sea dikes in central and northern Vietnam.

THE EL NIÑO EFFECT

El Niño is an ocean current that causes dramatic changes in the weather across the world, resulting in torrential rain and flooding in many countries.

Climate changes

El Niño is an ocean current that occurs every few years off the coast of Peru at Christmas. El Niño is Spanish for "the boy," or "the Christ child."

The current is a movement of warm water from the western side of the Pacific Ocean to the eastern side. The storm clouds that form over the warm water near Indonesia move across the ocean to the coasts of South and Central America, causing sudden, heavy downpours.

The effects of El Niño are felt all over the world. It has caused not only floods, but also **droughts** in Africa and Australia. It was also responsible for the dry conditions that led to forest fires in Indonesia in 1997 and a choking smog that spread to the rest of the region.

Global warming

Air pollution is making the world's climate warmer. This is called global warming. Scientists agree that global warming will result in dramatic changes in the world's weather, causing drought and famine in some areas and torrential rain and flooding in others. The ice caps of the north and south poles are slowly melting because of these changes (above). If this continues, sea levels will rise, flooding low-lying land around the world. Global warming will also intensify the effects of El Niño, bringing more dramatic changes to the weather.

► *The forest fires in Indonesia in 1997 were partly the result of El Niño.*

Americas 1997–98
El Niño at work

In 1997, El Niño began unusually early. From April 1997 through the first half of 1998, its terrible effects were felt by countries along the Pacific coastlines of North and South America.

Bolivia, Ecuador, and Peru were hit hard by weather. **States of emergency** were declared after deadly hurricanes and torrential rain swept across these countries. In Bolivia, heavy rain caused a mudslide that killed at least 40 people at a gold mine.

Heavy rain in Ecuador caused landslides that killed 100 people. Flooded rivers washed away whole villages, and bridges, roads, and **sewers** were badly damaged.

In Peru, floods and mudslides affected 234,000 people and claimed 137 lives between December 1997 and February 1998.

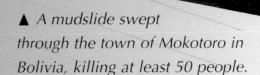

▲ A mudslide swept through the town of Mokotoro in Bolivia, killing at least 50 people.

Aid in the form of clothes, blankets, tents, medicine, clean water, and food was distributed to the affected people in these countries. Supplies had to be airlifted into areas cut off by flood waters. In some places, relief agencies helped to strengthen flood defenses that had been damaged, such as dikes along rivers.

◄ People in the Peruvian town of Ica wade through the deep, muddy water that flooded their homes.

11

FLOOD RESPONSE

Rescue teams are sent in as soon as news of a flood breaks. If the disaster is too large for them to handle, the government appeals for outside help.

Appeal for aid

When the effects of high tides, heavy rain, and powerful storms can be predicted, flood warnings can be given on radio and television. These warnings allow people to escape to safety before the flood arrives.

But if the flood takes an area by surprise, people may be unprepared for the rising waters, and many lives may be lost.

Rescue teams respond immediately. They rescue people trapped in the water or stranded on high ground or rooftops.

Governments often ask the **United Nations** (UN) and the **Red Cross** for help. These groups play an important role in coordinating the response to a disaster and may make an urgent appeal, or call, to the countries of the world to send aid supplies.

▲ *Boats were used to rescue people trapped in their homes when floods hit Texas in 1990.*

At greater risk

Many poor people live in **shantytowns** (left) on the edges of large cities and use whatever materials they can find to build their homes. These areas are often at the greatest risk of flooding. The homes and offices of the rich are often built on higher ground that is not threatened by flood water. When a flood strikes, the water easily carries away poor people's homes.

Azerbaijan 1997

Appealing for aid

In June 1997, heavy rain caused several rivers in Azerbaijan to overflow their banks. Homes in one area of the country were battered by hailstones the size of tennis balls that destroyed roofs and let rain into buildings. The government tried to help people in the affected areas, but it had to make an appeal for international aid because of its lack of resources.

A second wave of freak weather struck in early July, and more than seven times the average monthly rainfall fell in just three days. This was followed by more heavy rain in August, adding to the damage. Throughout the crisis, the country's government, the United Nations, the Red Cross, and other relief agencies worked together to help victims.

▲ *A woman stands in front of her flooded home in the village of Pechnoie.*

▼ *The flooding affected both the country's people and its industries, such as this oil field.*

The relief agencies gave out more than 30,000 food parcels to elderly people, and a further 210,000 parcels were given to other flood victims. Repairs to homes, hospitals, schools, and other important buildings were completed with the help of money donated by various relief agencies.

THE RESCUE EFFORT

Once survivors of a flood are rescued and taken to safety, they need shelter, food, and dry clothes.

Reaching the victims

Rescue teams use boats to reach people stranded by rising waters, but the boats may be too small to carry many people.

Sometimes the flood waters cover hundreds of square miles of land. Thousands of rescue workers are needed to cover such a vast area, and people may have to fend for themselves until help arrives.

Helicopters are sometimes used to pick up survivors stranded on high ground or in the branches of trees. Helicopters can search large areas quickly, which makes them very useful for directing the rescue effort and assessing the scale of the disaster.

While the survivors are being rescued, authorities set up relief camps and medical centers where people can stay until the emergency is over and they can return to what is left of their homes.

▲ A helicopter hovers as a person stranded by the rising flood water is lifted to safety.

Assessing the disaster

Relief agencies have teams of people who are specially trained to go to the scene of an emergency and assess what kind of help is needed. Once a call for help has been received, emergency teams travel out to the disaster area. The report they send back gives agencies a picture of the number of people affected, the condition of the roads and railroads, and the supplies needed, such as food and medicine.

Poland 1997

The Oder overflows

In July 1997, the Oder River over-flowed, flooding large parts of central and eastern Europe. Poland was one of the countries most affected. By August 1997, 55 people had died, and 142,000 others had been evacuated from their homes.

The rescue operation was led by the Polish government, who sent in the army, firefighters, and police with **amphibious** vehicles, helicopters, planes, and boats. Rescue teams also arrived from other European countries, including Germany, Switzerland, the Ukraine (part of the former **Soviet Union**), and Hungary, in an international effort.

▲ *The Oder River in flood. This image from the air shows the scale of the disaster.*

The suffering of the flood victims lasted well into the following year, when buildings still had water in them. But with donations from the **European Union**, homes, schools, and health centers were repaired.

Red Cross worker Thierry Le Goff said:

❝The effects of the summer floods will be felt for years to come. Our immediate concern is that winter is coming, and the most vulnerable families will not be able to return to acceptable living conditions without outside help.**❞**

Flood damage to homes left thousands of people living in miserable conditions.

SHIPPING IN SUPPLIES

Relief agencies work quickly to plan the best way to send relief supplies to the disaster area.

Transporting aid

Relief agencies have stockpiles of supplies for use in time of disaster, including tents, blankets, buckets, shovels, plastic sheets, pots and pans, electricity generators, water tanks, clothes, medical supplies, and food. These items are stored in huge warehouses that are often near airports, shipping ports, or train stations.

The most urgently needed items, such as tents, blankets, and medical supplies, are flown directly to the disaster area. But only small amounts of aid—about 27.5 tons (25 t)—can be transported by plane, which makes many flights necessary.

Large ships carrying thousands of tons of aid may take weeks to sail to a port in the affected country. Once the ships dock, supplies are loaded onto trains or trucks.

Flood waters may have washed away bridges or damaged roads, making it difficult to get people the relief that they need.

Emergency donations

Governments may send aid supplies themselves or donate money to relief agencies involved in the relief effort. The public may also want to give money to help flood victims. This money is spent on renting or buying trucks; fuel for the trucks; transporting supplies by ship; helicopter services (above); repairing damaged roads or bridges; buying relief supplies; and sending trained relief workers to the disaster area.

◄ *In Chad, trucks carrying food cross a temporary bridge after the river washed away the bridge.*

Africa 1997–98
Sending in aid

Flooding in eastern Africa at the end of 1997 and beginning of 1998 affected large areas of Uganda, Kenya, Somalia, Ethiopia, Sudan, Djibouti, and Eritrea. The region was already facing food shortages because of drought.

This crisis situation led to a huge international relief effort involving the governments of the countries affected, the Red Cross, the United Nations, and other relief agencies.

Cooperation between the countries and agencies involved was essential if the rescue effort was to be a success. For example, aid supplies shipped to the Kenyan port of Mombassa had to travel by road or railroad through Kenya to reach Uganda.

▲ *The village of Rhoka in Kenya was flooded when the Tana River overflowed.*

Roads and railroads in many of the countries were damaged, so airlifts and airdrops were often the only quick way of reaching tens of thousands of flood victims. In some areas, relief agencies used **Hercules** transport planes to fly in relief supplies until the roads were usable again. These planes flew in supplies for weeks on end. Boats were also used to reach people stranded on islands of high ground in remote areas.

◄ *Trucks slowly make their way through a flooded road in Kenya.*

FOOD SHORTAGES

A flood destroys crops and drowns farm animals. This causes food shortages after a flood that may lead to famine.

Food aid

Many people make a living by farming the land. The crops a farmer grows provide food for the family and a source of money when sold at the local market.

Floods ruin farmers' crops and food supplies, leaving people without anything to eat. People sometimes lose everything they own in a flood, leaving them with nothing to sell to buy food.

In coastal areas, a flood from the ocean leaves the ground salty and unsuitable for growing crops. Eventually, the rain washes the salt away, allowing crops to grow again, but this takes time.

Many flood victims need food aid to survive. They may need emergency supplies if their food supplies have been destroyed and long-term aid until their land is able to grow crops again.

World Food Program

The United Nations has a department called the World Food Program (WFP) that helps to coordinate food aid in emergencies. The WFP appeals to the world for food, and countries that have more than they need donate supplies. It is important that the food fits the diet of the people who need it. For example, many people in Africa and Asia eat corn or rice as their main diet. Often, the WFP buys food from countries in the region of the flooding. This saves time and money when transporting supplies (above) to victims of floods.

▼ *This field, flooded by saltwater from the sea, cannot support crops.*

North Korea 1995–96

Food and floods

Flooding in North Korea in August 1995 covered one-third of the country's farmland with water and destroyed most of its crops.

The relief operation that followed included the delivery of thousands of tons of rice, corn, and soybeans to the people most affected.

People had just begun to rebuild their lives when disaster struck again. There was more heavy rain and more flooding in July and August 1996, damaging the next harvest. The homes of nearly 150,000 people were swept away by the flood water, and people faced another year of food shortages.

▲ *People receiving food aid from a WFP distribution center in Huichon in North Korea.*

Geoff Dennis of the Red Cross surveys the damage caused by the floods.

Many people, especially children, suffered from **malnutrition**. They were treated by Red Cross medical teams and given food sent from other countries. Red Cross representative Geoff Dennis said:

"People lost everything. Many were rescued from higher ground, having escaped with only the clothes on their backs. The Red Cross [and other agencies] have carried out a remarkable job, saving lives and relieving the suffering of many. . . .**"**

DIRTY WATERS

Clean drinking water is essential for life. During a flood, however, streams and wells are dirtied by flood waters.

Water for life

In an emergency, it is important that survivors are provided with a supply of clean drinking water as soon as possible.

During a flood, water supplies become muddy with the dirt carried in the water. Drains and sewers overflow, and the material they carry leaks into streams and wells, contaminating them.

Dirty water contains germs that cause disease. Cholera is a life-threatening disease that can easily be passed from person to person. In relief camps, it is essential that relief agencies set up proper toilet facilities to prevent the spread of disease.

Floods from the sea also spoil water supplies. The salt from the sea has to be removed from the water before it is drinkable again.

Relief agencies help communities to clean up their water supplies and provide new sources of clean water by digging wells.

▲ A Bangladeshi woman stands at a well surrounded by rising flood water.

Fighting disease

In addition to treating the injured, relief agencies work to fight disease. **Médecins Sans Frontières** (MSF) sends doctors, nurses, and health workers to help flood victims. Medical workers advise on setting up toilets, treat water to make it drinkable again, and give medicine to people suffering from fever, diarrhea, and other illnesses.

In relief camps, disease spreads quickly between people living close together. Medical workers can help prevent some diseases by giving vaccinations—injections of medicine that keep flood victims from becoming sick.

DRC 1998
Preventing disease

In 1998, heavy rainfall caused the Congo River and the rivers that feed it to overflow their banks and flood an area thousands of miles wide in the Democratic Republic of Congo (DRC). One of the worst effects of the flood was the outbreak of disease—as many as one million people were expected to become sick from drinking dirty water.

Elderly people, children, and those weakened by lack of food were particularly at risk. The government and relief agencies were worried that an outbreak of cholera in Kisangani, DRC's largest northern city, could spread to other parts of the country.

People were also threatened by malaria, a disease spread by mosquitoes, which breed over large areas of stagnant water.

▲ People wade through a flooded street after the Congo River overflowed.

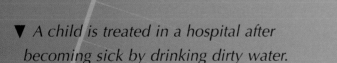
▼ A child is treated in a hospital after becoming sick by drinking dirty water.

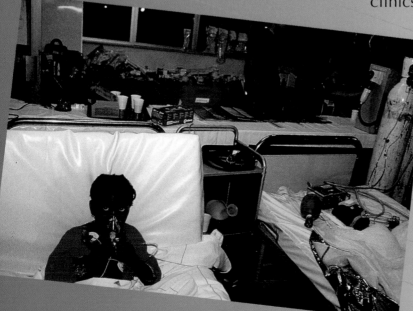

Relief agencies shipped in supplies to clinics and hospitals across the DRC, including 10,000 anti-cholera vaccines; 50,000 syringes for giving injections; 200,000 packs of salts to make medicinal drinks for people with diarrhea; 23,000 square feet (2,000 sq m) of plastic sheeting for beds; 500 large pots for boiling water; water purification tablets; and 500 shovels.

DISAPPEARING FORESTS

Large numbers of trees are constantly being cut down to clear land for farming and to supply wood for timber. This deforestation can lead to serious flooding.

Flooding and landslides

Without trees, land is at a greater risk from flooding. Trees shield the land from sudden downpours, and their roots absorb water, helping it to soak into the ground. Without trees, water **erodes** the soil, increasing the risk of flooding.

Deforestation also increases the risk of landslides. After heavy rain, the soil becomes **saturated** with water and begins to slide downhill. Without trees, there is no natural barrier to the moving soil.

Deforestation is a serious problem in many countries. Relief agencies encourage local people to plant new trees to replace the ones that are cut down. By doing this, people protect their land from erosion and protect themselves from the risk of flooding and landslides.

▲ *When this forest was destroyed, thousands of tons of soil were washed away by rain.*

Paying the price

Some governments and international banks have lent money to **developing countries** for projects that destroy forests. These include projects to build dams and large farms to grow cash crops (left). Often, these projects do not benefit local people; they benefit only the large companies that own the farms or build the dams. These projects put people at a greater risk from flooding because of the lack of trees.

Haiti 1997

Planting trees for the future

Haiti is the poorest country in the Caribbean. It has two large mountain ranges, where farmers have cleared forests to grow food crops.

Haiti has heavy downpours of rain between May and November, and toward the end of the rainy season it is often hit by **hurricanes**. Deforestation on the mountain slopes has eroded the soil, increasing the risk of flooding in the valleys below.

But a project has recently been started that encourages children to replant trees on bare hillsides to prevent flooding problems. It is run by a Haitian **environmental agency** and is supported by the Save the Children Fund agency.

▲ *A hillside in Haiti shows signs of erosion after the trees were cut down.*

Benita, one of the children involved with the tree-planting project, said:

"We were told about the importance of trees to our environment, shown how to water them and how to protect them from animals that want to eat them. . . . Now if I see someone cutting down a tree, I tell them that their actions affect us all.**"**

Fourteen-year-old Benita shows off her seedlings, which will reforest the hillsides.

23

RETURNING HOME

When flood water has subsided, people can return to their homes. But they may need help to start again.

Picking up the pieces

Flood victims face many difficulties when they return home. Their houses may have been torn down by the rushing water, their wells contaminated by dirty water, and their crops and animals killed. Everything they owned and worked for may be damaged or lost. But within days, people start picking up the pieces of their lives and repairing their homes or those of neighbors.

Many people are too poor to replace the things they lost in the flood, so governments and relief agencies help people until they are able to carry on without aid. Governments and agencies give out seeds for planting the next crop, or farm tools to work the land. Flood victims may continue to receive food aid until the next harvest.

Loans to rebuild

Some flood victims need loans to restart local businesses such as basket weaving, pottery, or cloth-making. People in many countries fish for a living, and fishermen may need new boats and nets. A loan of money from a bank must be repaid with interest. Interest is an extra amount that people pay in addition to the money they have borrowed. Relief agencies often give loans without interest. These free loans allow people to buy what they need and then pay back the money over a period of time in amounts that they can afford.

◄ *Villagers in the Philippines clear away the mess after a flash flood caused by deforestation.*

Somalia 1997–98

Makeshift camps

Flooding began in this African country in October 1997 and continued well into 1998. By February 1998, nearly 2,500 people had been killed and about one million others desperately needed help. Crops were underwater, and as food supplies were used up, the risk of famine was great. To make sure people were fed, relief agencies gave food aid to flood victims who had gathered together in makeshift camps on tiny patches of dry land.

The mother of a group of children made homeless by the flood told how they gathered materials for their makeshift hut:

▲ *A shot from the air shows a Somali village and surrounding fields swamped by the rising water.*

"We gathered everything we could—pieces of metal sheeting, boards, uprooted bushes, and cardboard floating in the water."

Flood victims had no clean drinking water and were surviving on fish and mangoes. Mosquitoes were spreading malaria. The Red Crescent sprayed the village with **insecticides** to kill the mosquitoes and set up a system to provide clean water.

▶ *A worker sprays insecticide over mosquito breeding areas.*

FLOOD DEFENSES

Countries at risk from flooding build flood defenses to hold back the water. But this can be expensive, and some countries cannot afford this protection.

Flood defenses

River banks can be strengthened or raised in certain places. For example, high banks or levees have been built along the Mississippi River to protect people from floods. Barriers are built across rivers to protect cities from flooding. Because these defenses are expensive, relief agencies help poorer countries build them. River banks are raised and **spillways** are dug to divert high water from where it would cause the most damage.

Many countries have storm shelters where people can go if waters start rising. These shelters are built of brick and plaster and are raised on columns to withstand wind, rain, and flood water.

▲ *Bangladeshi women work to build an embankment.*

Repairing the damage

Floods damage roads and bridges, weaken buildings, wash away fences and trees, and leave debris everywhere. Repairing large structures takes time and effort, and not all building materials are available locally. Relief agencies can help by sending materials, such as concrete and bricks, to the affected area. But it is usually local people who clean up the mess after the flood and organize the needed repairs (left). If necessary, relief agencies support flood victims with cash-for-work plans that pay people for the repair work they do.

Bangladesh 1997

Cyclone shelters

Bangladesh is a low-lying country in Asia that is often hit by tropical storms called cyclones. Cyclones whip up huge waves at sea that cause heavy damage and can kill many people when they come ashore. A cyclone in 1991, for example, killed 13,000 people. In May 1997, another cyclone struck Bangladesh. It was as powerful as the 1991 storm and destroyed or damaged 400,000 homes, though it killed fewer people; about 200 people died. Many people took refuge in cyclone shelters while the storm raged. Many of these shelters were built with help from relief agencies such as ACTIONAID.

▲ Flooding caused by a cyclone. Every year, these powerful storms threaten Bangladesh.

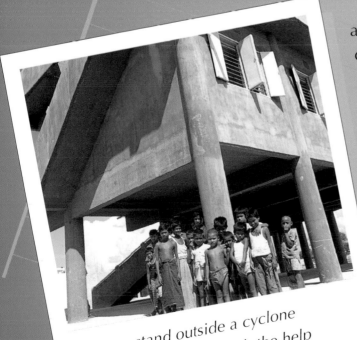

Children stand outside a cyclone shelter that was built with the help of relief agencies.

Nur Begum and her family run a small roadside restaurant serving customers rotis (a round, flat bread) and tea. They took refuge in a shelter when the cyclone hit:

"We had to stay there for two days because the area became flooded with seawater. The storm damaged the roof of our roadside restaurant and the oven we used to cook the rotis."

MANAGING FLOODS

A plan of action helps countries that flood frequently to react swiftly when disaster strikes.

Action plans

Countries all over the world are affected by natural disasters such as floods, earthquakes, droughts, and volcanic eruptions.

For people who live in these countries, the threat of natural disasters is a part of everyday life, so it is important that they know what to do if disaster strikes. Relief agencies and governments work together to draw up disaster rescue plans.

These plans start by looking at the hazards a country faces and producing a map of the areas most at risk. A system for warning people of the arrival of a disaster is set up. Emergency services are taught what to do if disaster strikes, such as how to reach flood victims and how to treat them for **hypothermia**. Measures are taken to limit the effects of a flood; these measures include the building of storm shelters.

Relief agencies and governments also tell people about the work that is being done to protect them and give them advice on what to do if a flood strikes.

Getting ready

Here are some of the things people are advised to do if their area is hit by a flood: listen to the radio for news about the flood and advice on what to do; disconnect televisions and other electrical appliances; move valuable belongings and clothes out of reach of the water; move vehicles and farm animals to high ground; prevent pollution by moving dangerous chemicals such as insecticides to a safe place; turn off electricity and gas sources; lock windows and doors when leaving home; return home only when the water level has subsided; and do not wander around flooded areas alone.

◀ *A Chinese woman is helped to safety by soldiers.*

Pacific Islands 1998
Reducing the damage

The islands of the South Pacific, such as the Solomon Islands, Cook Islands, Fiji, and Papua New Guinea, are beautiful islands with palm-fringed beaches. But they are regularly threatened by disasters that can kill people and destroy homes.

Cyclones are the most common disasters and have the most damaging effect. They can create huge waves at sea that crash onto the shore, damaging or destroying everything in their path. The high winds also cause damage, and dangerous mudslides in hilly areas may follow the heavy rains.

▶ *The man-made reef around Kurumba Island in the Maldives is designed to protect the island from rising sea levels.*

▼ *Upolu Island in western Samoa is lashed by high winds and huge waves during a powerful tropical storm.*

In 1994, the island countries and the United Nations worked together to reduce the effects of natural disasters in the area. They set up a plan for disaster management called the South Pacific Disaster Reduction Program, which includes flood warnings and forecasting, training of officials, education for the public on what to do during disasters, and closer contact between the islands of the South Pacific.

HOW YOU CAN HELP

Floods are a danger in many countries, large and small, rich and poor. Sometimes people lose everything they own in a flood.

● Collect newspaper reports about floods and mark on a map where they happened. Did relief agencies send supplies to the country affected?

● Find out about a relief agency you would like to help. With your friends, collect unwanted books, clothes, and blankets, and donate them to your chosen charity.

● You might like to raise money for your charity by organizing a fund-raising activity. A sponsored bike ride or run is fun for everyone. Maybe your entire school could be involved. You could design your own sponsorship forms and provide information about how the money will be spent.

Finding out more

Write to relief agencies or visit their web sites to find out about their work and how you can help.

American Red Cross
6th Floor
8111 Gatehouse Road
Falls Church, VA 22042
http://www.redcross.org/

The Canadian Red Cross Society
1800 Alta Vista Drive
Ottawa, ON K1G 4J5
http://www.redcross.ca/newbanner/
nonjava.htm

CAUSE Canada
P.O. Box 8100
Canmore, AB T1W 2T8
http://www.cause.ca/

International Relief Association
1823 East 17th Street
Suite 317
Santa Ana, CA 92705
http://www.ira-usa.org/

International Service Agencies
66 Canal Center Plaza
Suite 310
Alexandria, VA 22314
http://www.charity.org/

Oxfam America
26 West Street
Boston, MA 02111
http://www.oxfamamerica.org/

Save the Children
54 Wilton Road
Westport, CT 06880
http://www.savethechildren.org/

World Relief Corporation
P.O. Box WRC
Wheaton, IL 60189
http://www.worldrelief.org/